Halley's Comet

The last time it appeared people thought they'd be gassed! The next time it appears you'll be seventy-six years older! Right now it's hurtling back into our skies after around three-quarters of a century out in the frozen depths of space!

It is, of course, Halley's Comet and this book explains:

What it is

*

When and where it can best be seen

*

Who Edmond Halley was

*

And why you just MUST NOT miss it!

Your indispensable guide to the world's most famous comet.

Halley's Comet

Peter Wragg

Illustrated by Jeremy Ford
Cartoons by Taffy Davies

KNIGHT BOOKS
Hodder and Stoughton

To Simon and James, and all children everywhere

Text copyright © 1985 Victorama Ltd.
Illustrations copyright © 1985 Hodder & Stoughton Ltd.
First published by Knight Books 1985
Third impression 1986

British Library C.I.P.

Wragg, Peter
  Halley's Comet.
  1. Halley's comet – Juvenile literature
  I. Title   II. Ford, Jeremy   III. Davies, Taffy
  523.6′4   QB723.H2

  ISBN 0 340 38087 X

Printed and bound in Great Britain for
Hodder and Stoughton Paperbacks, a
division of Hodder and Stoughton Ltd.,
Mill Road, Dunton Green, Sevenoaks,
Kent (Editorial Office: 47 Bedford
Square, London, WC1 3DP) by
Richard Clay (The Chaucer Press) Ltd.,
Bungay, Suffolk. Photoset by
Rowland Phototypesetting Ltd.,
Bury St Edmunds, Suffolk.

Contents

Illustration Acknowledgements

Page 16 – *The spaceprobe 'Giotto' on its way to explore the head of Halley's Comet*; based on picture by British Aerospace.

Page 28 – *Where to look for Halley's Comet in the Northern Hemisphere, 50° N in 1986*; adapted from diagram from THE COMET HALLEY HANDBOOK, An Observer's Guide, Second Edition by Donald K Yeomans (published by NASA – Jet Propulsion Laboratory, California Institute of Technology, Pasadena, California).

Page 32 – *Where to look for Halley's Comet in the Southern Hemisphere, 30° S in 1986*; based on diagram from THE COMET HALLEY HANDBOOK as above.

Page 36 – *The structure of the head of Halley's Comet; based on drawing by Jeff Simms*, © copyright The Times Newspapers Ltd., Sunday Times Magazine 30.12.84 p. 20.

Page 61 – *The path of Halley's Comet in the sky during November 1985 – May 1986*; based on diagram from THE COMET HALLEY HANDBOOK as above.

Introduction

For tens of thousands of years men have stood outside at night and looked up at the stars above their heads. For a long time they probably saw nothing more than thousands of random twinkling bodies, to which they gave names. They may have even thought that the stars they saw could affect their lives. But after a while they began to realise something more definite: that what they saw in the sky was predictable; there was a pattern to it. The stars seemed to move regularly around the Earth, as did the Sun and the Moon. Putting these facts together, they came to the conclusion that the Earth was at the centre of the universe.

Man must, at some point, have noticed that some of the heavenly bodies he saw were recognisably different from others but it was not until he had been civilised for some time that he began to realise that some of them did not follow regular paths but had hiccups in their movements, or slowed down in their paths across the sky. It was the brilliant Polish astronomer and mathematician, Niklas Koppernigk (usually known by his Latin name – Copernicus) who put forward the theory that the Earth is not the centre of the universe, but is just one of a number of planets that move around the Sun. Although his ideas were taught in the universities of the time, they were treated as just another explanation for the movements of the stars. They were not really taken seriously until quite a few years after his death in 1543, when the Catholic Church began to take a particular interest. Copernicus's ideas denied a lot of what the Church had been teaching and as a result in 1616 they were denounced and outlawed. They were not accepted by the Church until 1822, although by this time scientists and mathematicians had seen much of what he had predicted *proved* by the astronomical telescope and the mathematical theories of Isaac Newton.

Apart from the patterns that man observed, he also saw things in the sky that he could *not* explain easily. For example, at times all or part of the Sun would disappear. Sometimes the same thing would happen to the Moon. We now know that this is an eclipse; a solar eclipse is when the Moon comes between the Earth and the Sun; a lunar eclipse is when the Earth is between the Sun and the Moon. Man also saw shooting stars – now called meteors – that made brilliant streaks across the sky and then disappeared. And finally, there were the comets – mysterious, different and seemingly unpredictable – weird heavenly bodies that seemed to wander around space with no direction or pattern. It is about comets, and one comet in particular, that this book has been written.

Halley's Comet has been known to man since 240 BC, but it is named after Edmond Halley, a great seventeenth-century astronomer, as he was the first man to work out that its movements followed a regular pattern. It appears every seventy-five to seventy-eight years, which means that most of us only get one chance to see it in our lifetime. That, and its historical fame, is why everyone is getting so excited about its appearance this year!

You will see lots about Halley's Comet in the newspapers and on the television. This book explains what it is and how scientists will be tracking it; it tells you how to watch it and record your observations; and it explains who Edmond Halley was and why he is important, and gives you lots of useful astronomical background information. It also contains a number of words you may not have seen before. Where possible I have tried to explain their meaning in the text, but there is a list of words at the back that I hope will explain anything you do not understand. Finally, at the end of each chapter is a MEGA-TEASER; the answers – should you need them! – are near the back.

1

International Comet Watch

Halley's Comet is one of the brightest, most spectacular and most regular of all the comets. It will be seen in the sky towards the end of 1985 and during the first few months of 1986, after which it will disappear and will not be seen again for another seventy-six years. Its appearances have been recorded regularly every seventy-five to seventy-eight years since 240 BC and as this may be your only chance to see it, make sure you don't waste the opportunity! Of course, if you live to be very old you may get another chance. How old will you be when it next appears?

The Comet's current visit will last about four and

a half months, though it will not be visible for the whole of that time. It will appear first as a small, bright speck in the sky, probably only visible at night. But as time goes on it will become brighter, and its tail will become visible. If we are very lucky it will be bright enough to be seen in the daytime.

As you will see when you reach the next chapter, the best place to watch the Comet is from a high hilltop. During the time the Comet is visible, hilltops are likely to be crowded with watchers! Some of them will be professionals, but most of them will be keen amateurs, perhaps like yourself. Talk to them if you can; you may learn a great deal from them, and usually they will be only too keen to help you. They should be able to tell you exactly where to look, and may even let you use some of their equipment. They may also tell you if there is a local astronomical society, when it meets, and whether it has a junior section. From them, you might be able to learn much more about what can be seen in the sky, and what interesting events can be expected in the near future.

Enthusiastic amateurs will not be the only watchers. Comets are still considered to be among the most mysterious of the objects that can be observed in space, and scientists all over the world are getting very excited about the reappearance of Halley's Comet. In October 1982 the Comet had been spotted already as it gradually moved towards us by a team of astronomers in America, using special equipment and a huge 5.08 metre telescope on top of the Palomar mountain in California. Scientists will be watching everything that the Comet does as it passes through our part of the solar system, and the nearer that it gets the more they can find out about it. They are interested in how it moves, why it should have such an enormous orbit, what it is made of, why its tail always points away from the Sun, how long it will last, and in so many other questions that it would be almost impossible to list them. Every observatory throughout the world will spend some of its time watching the slow, majestic progress of Halley's Comet across the sky.

How scientists will watch the Comet

There are a number of ways in which scientists can study a comet. Of course, simply to watch it gives a fair amount of information, and since there will be many millions of eyes in many thousands of places watching the progress of Halley's Comet, a great deal should be learnt.

Because you can see a comet, this means that it must be giving off light. This occurs as a result of the reflection of sunlight and because certain gaseous molecules fluoresce under the action of solar radiation, and another way in which scientists can investigate the Comet is by looking at the light that comes from it. This is called *spectrographic analysis*, and means comparing the light from the Comet with light from other known substances. It is a very complicated task, but should enable scientists to find out in great detail what the Comet is made of, why it has a 'coma', and why it has a tail. They will not only be looking at the Comet by means of visible light but also by infrared and ultraviolet light, as well as studying it by using radio waves. This will be done from the ground, from high-flying aircraft, from satellites that are already orbiting the Earth and from spacecraft launched into deep space.

One problem that we have in looking at anything from Earth is created by the atmosphere around us; what we see is altered by the gases in the air, the amount of water that the air contains, and the temperature of the air around us. (This is why most astronomical observatories are built on hills; there is less atmosphere between them and what they are looking at!) To avoid this problem the best place from which to observe anything is from where there is no atmosphere – in outer space.

By January 1985 one satellite had been launched expressly to investigate the Comet, and many of the satellites that are already in space will look very closely at the Comet as it passes us, and use their many sensors to find out as much as they can about it. In all, five spacecraft have been or will be launched just to look at Halley's Comet – one from Europe, two from Japan and two from Russia. The Americans have sent a spacecraft called *ICE* (International Comet Explorer) to study a comet called Giacobini-Zinner in September 1985, and this will go on to Halley's Comet in March 1986. The Russians have launched two spacecraft called the *Vega* probes. The one that British scientists have helped design is called *Giotto*, after the thirteenth-century Italian painter Giotto di Bondone. Giotto saw Halley's Comet in the year 1301, and used it to represent the Star of Bethlehem in a painting of the Nativity. *Giotto*, which was built mainly in Bristol, England, was launched during July 1985. The first Russian spacecraft will reach the Comet on or around 6 March 1986, and the second on or around 9 March. The Japanese satellites should be near the Comet on 8 March. The information they pick up from being so close to the Comet will be sent back to the Earth, and it is hoped that they will be able to pinpoint accurately the 'head' of the Comet. The plan is then to try to send *Giotto* towards the Comet's head. There is speculation as to whether the spaceprobe will survive this encounter intact as it will suffer some micrometeroid damage, but if scientists can get it within 500 kilometres of the Comet they will consider the mission successful. The launching of these spacecraft is an indication of the extent to which scientists all over the world are willing to co-operate to find out as much as they can about the Comet.

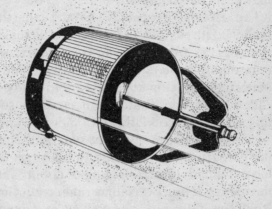

The space probe 'Giotto' on its way to explore the head of Halley's Comet

To launch spacecraft is a very expensive business and, although once up they will provide scientists with a great deal of information, this is not the only way that scientists can study the Comet. All of the great observatories on Earth will at one time or another be training their telescopes on it, and telescopes carried in high-flying aeroplanes will also be used. The Anglo-Australian Telescope on Siding Spring Mountain, New South Wales, Australia, is in a very good position to observe the Comet. Other good locations for observation in the Southern Hemisphere are the west coast of Madagascar, the south-west African desert (Maun, Botswana), the Andes Mountains (Arequipa, Peru; La Quiaca, Argentina) and the central desert of Australia (Alice Springs and Mundiwindi). The Comet will be most clearly visible during April 1986 at these locations.

The last time that Halley's Comet came this close to the Earth was in 1910 (when it actually came even closer). Nowadays we can find out so much more about the heavenly bodies that come near to our planet that it is hoped that we may be able to solve some of the mysteries of these unusual wanderers in deep space.

In order to get as much information as possible, many scientists have decided to get together and pool all their information. So far, about 875 astronomers in forty-seven different countries have decided to take part, and they have named thirty-one Halley Watch days when people all over the world will be watching the Comet at the same time. With all the information that they will assemble, they hope to find out much more about what the different parts of a comet are made of, the way in which a comet affects the planets that it passes, and the way in which its tail grows and lessens.

Each country taking part has an International Halley Watch (IHW) leader, whose job is to collect all the information from all of his observers, and to keep them informed of anything unusual that anyone in any other country has noticed. They will also pass on any information they get to the radio and television services, so that the information can be made known to the general public. Eventually they hope to publish a book, possibly accompanied by a collection of photographs taken from the ground, the air and the spacecraft. They may even make a video using all the available information and the best photographs.

In Britain, National Astronomy week has been planned to coincide with the first period of reasonable visibility of the Comet – from November 9 to 16 – when it will appear near the Pleiades star cluster. Another point worth noting is that a nationwide *Halley Hotline* has been launched, by British Aerospace in conjunction with the Halley's Comet Society and British Telecom. Just by dialling a phone number you can get regularly updated information on the Comet and the progress of the Giotto programme. Here are the numbers to ring:

London	01-790 3400
Birmingham	021-355-6144
Glasgow	041-552-6300
Liverpool	051-236-8474
Leeds	0532-8013
Bristol	0272-279494
Cardiff	0222-399855
Belfast	0232-230505
Manchester	061-246-8061

Altogether, this is likely to be one of the most interesting and well co-ordinated scientific events that has happened for a very long time.

Mega-Teaser 1

What would happen if we should get too close to the Comet, or even if it should hit our planet?
(For the answer, turn to page 78.)

2

How you can Comet Watch

Don't be discouraged from having a go yourself at studying Halley's Comet just because, having read the last chapter, you now have an idea of the tremendous amount of money and resources that countries all over the world are using to do this. You may well say to yourself: 'Well, I haven't got a telescope, and I can't afford even the cheapest pair of binoculars. What is the point of my going out to look at it? I'm not going to be able to help in any way!' But it is worth remembering that Halley's Comet was first noticed by people who had no aid to their vision – no telescopes or binoculars to use, or anything of that sort. The naked eye still has great advantages over the use of additional optical aids because it can see over a wide area of the sky all at once, so what you may lose in detail you will gain in many other ways. With a telescope or binoculars you will only be able to focus on a small part of the Comet, and you may well miss what is happening in other parts of the sky.

There are often problems involved in trying to look for unusual objects in the sky. To begin with, there are sometimes clouds about which make it difficult to see the stars at all. Secondly, many towns are brightly lit at night, and the glow from the street-lights and factories makes it difficult to see things that are close to the horizon. So, when you go out to see Halley's Comet, remember these points:

1. Choose a clear, cloudless night.

2. Try to avoid looking for it in areas where there is the glow from a big city nearby. If you can get away from the city, make sure that it is not between you and the Comet.

3. You will get by far the best sighting in 1986 if you live south of the equator – at times the Comet will be almost directly overhead, and will move across the horizon from due east to almost due west. However, whichever side of the world you view from, try to get as high up as you can; find a hill that faces south where there are no obstructions between you and the path of the Comet.

4. Although the Comet should eventually be clear-

ly visible to the naked eye, especially in the middle of its period, if you are able to take with you some sort of optical aid – a telescope or binoculars – it will help you to study the detail better.

5. A WARNING! Whatever you do, do not attempt to look for the Comet in daytime through a telescope or binoculars! A small mistake, such as focusing on the Sun accidentally, could seriously damage your eyes.

6. (A sneaky suggestion!) Try to get your parents interested in what you are doing. They may then be willing to drive you far out into the countryside, and stand for hours on a hilltop looking for the Comet. With a little bit of persuasion, they might also take your friends with you – a lot of eyes are better than one pair – and they may even be willing to provide you with hot soup, sandwiches, etc. A midnight picnic could be good fun!

7. ANOTHER WARNING! Don't ever go out at night on your own, unless your parents know exactly where you are going, and what time you will be back. Always try to be fair to your parents, and return at the time you say you will.

Although optical aids are not essential to a study of the Comet, they will help you to study it in detail.

Binoculars

Probably the most common optical aid found in many homes is a pair of binoculars. These are

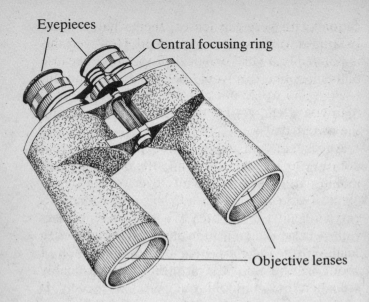

Eyepieces

Central focusing ring

Objective lenses

A pair of prismatic binoculars

generally only used to give you close-up magnification of objects a kilometre or so away, and they will magnify the object that you are looking at between four and twenty times. If you look at the binoculars that you are going to use, you will find on them somewhere a sign, such as '6 x 40'. The first number – six in this case – is the number of times that the object you are looking at will be increased in size. The second number – forty – is in many respects, the more important of the two. It tells you the diameter of the object lenses of the binoculars in millimetres. This is an indication of how much light the lenses are taking in, and obviously the bigger the lenses the brighter the image. You can probably work out that if you have a very small magnifi-

22

cation, with very big lenses, then what you are looking at will be very bright indeed. However, this is not really a very practical proposition because binoculars like this would be very heavy and unwieldy, and would not give you much more detail than you would get by looking at the Comet with the naked eye.

Another factor that you must bear in mind is that not only do binoculars magnify the object you are looking at, they also magnify every small movement of your hands or head. This means that it is very difficult to hold steady a pair of binoculars with a large magnification number focused on a small object. For most people, a magnification of about eight to ten is the most they can reasonably use when they are looking at objects in the sky. If your binoculars are more powerful than this, you will have to find a way of holding them steady, by resting them on a wall, on the roof of the car, or on a camera tripod which will fit binoculars.

If you are long-sighted or short-sighted and usually wear glasses, you will find that you do not need to wear them when looking through binoculars, even if one eye is stronger than the other. One of the lenses will have an adjustment on the eyepiece, and the binoculars will compensate for the lenses in your glasses if you adjust the focusing wheel in the middle.

Telescopes

There are two types of telescope that can easily be used by the amateur astronomer. The first, and oldest, type is the 'refracting' telescope. This uses

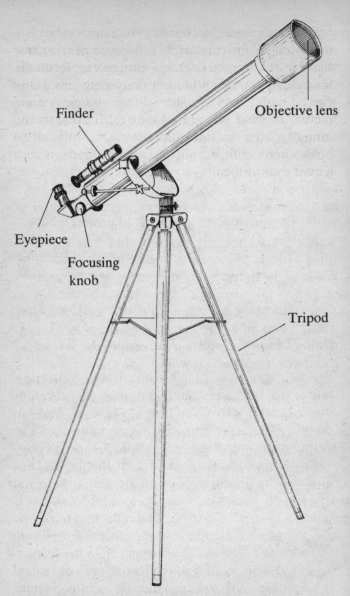

Finder

Objective lens

Eyepiece

Focusing
knob

Tripod

A refracting astronomical telescope

24

lenses in the same way that binoculars do but is a much longer instrument. It is the type of telescope that pirates and sea captains used to use! It usually has a high magnification, and has a big lens at the end to gather lots of light, so that you get a good picture of what you are looking at. It presents the same problem as binoculars, i.e. it is difficult to hold steady, but usually it can be fitted on to a tripod to hold it still.

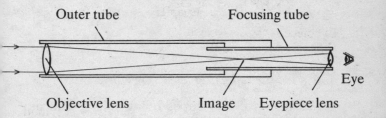

How a simple refracting telescope works

The other type of telescope is the 'reflecting' telescope. Instead of lenses this uses very carefully made curved mirrors to collect the light, and has one or two lenses to focus it into your eye. The main astronomical telescopes used in the big observatories around the world are of this type. They often have a little telescope on the side, to help you line up on what you want to look at, and this is called a 'finder' telescope. The reflecting telescope will give you a clearer and more detailed picture and a good one is usually cheaper than the refracting type. The main light-collecting mirror, called the primary mirror, is usually ten to fifteen centimetres across. The Anglo-Australian Telescope

25

has a primary mirror more than 380 centimetres across!

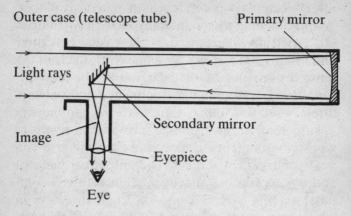

How a simple reflecting telescope works

You may see telescopes being sold specifically for viewing Halley's Comet. Binoculars really are best for beginners, but if you do want to invest in a telescope, contact your local astronomical society for advice.

If you are going to use a telescope or binoculars, take note of the following important warnings. It is not a good idea to spend the whole night gazing at the sky through them. Not only will it give you a very stiff neck, but it can also make your eyes very tired. Try not to use your telescope or binoculars for more than a few minutes at a time, and give your eyes a rest afterwards. Secondly, remember that telescopes and binoculars are precision scientific instruments. They will get damaged if you bash them against walls, or throw them in the boot of a car. They can be affected by damp, so if you have been outside on a cold night always leave them in a warm (not *hot*) place to dry out thoroughly before you use them again. Always put on the lens caps after use, and try not to leave them in dusty places. Avoid touching lenses and mirrors with anything at all, especially fingers and, if the casing gets dirty and muddy, do not use the same cloth to clean the lenses or mirrors as you used to wipe the mud off. Once any part of the lens is scratched it will always affect what you see. A simple, caring routine will ensure that the instruments are always ready to work at a moment's notice, and they will give you years of excellent service. The only other piece of equipment you may need to begin with is a compass, so that you can find the right direction in which to look. If you can find a compass that has degrees marked around the outside edge, even better.

When and where to look in the Northern Hemisphere

If you have an astronomical telescope, you should be able to pick out Halley's Comet during late October and November in the south-east and south. By December, you should be able to see it through binoculars in the south-west (this is why you need a compass) if you look for it about half-way between the horizon and the zenith. (This is the bit of the sky that is directly over the top of your head.) The time to look is between one and one-and-a-half hours after the Sun has gone down. Shortly after this it will disappear below the horizon.

By the beginning of 1986 it should be possible to

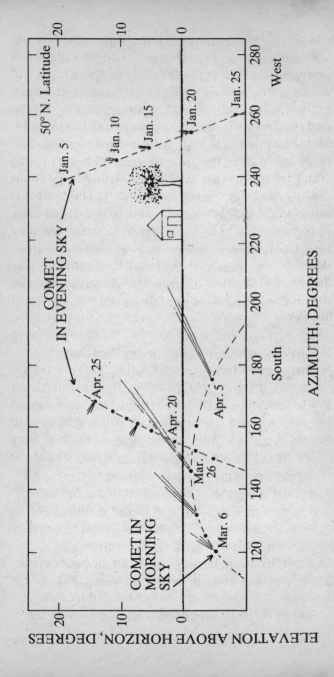

see the Comet just by using your eyes. Go out about the same time to see it. To begin with, it will be relatively high in the sky. As time goes on, it will get brighter and its tail will get longer, and each night it will appear slightly lower in the sky. By the end of January it will disappear below the horizon. However, *all is not lost*! Although you will have to give up 'comet-spotting' during February – this comet anyway – it should be possible in latitudes not too far north to see it in March. This time it is not at night that you will be able to see it, but early in the morning. The best time to look for it will be about one to one-and-a-half hours before sunrise. Because the Sun will be rising earlier each day during March, look in your daily paper to find the time for sunrise on the day before the one when you are going 'comet-spotting'. The times of sunrise are usually given near to the weather map, so you have two useful pieces of information together.

To begin with, the Comet will appear low on the horizon slightly to the south of the east mark on your compass. If you live in Britain or areas on similar latitudes (about 50°N) it will not be easy to see the Comet at this time unless it becomes very bright or its tail very long. Still, you may be able to

Where to look for Halley's Comet in the Northern Hemisphere (50° N Latitude) in 1986, when it will be most clearly visible. Comet positions are given for morning astronomical twilight or evening astronomical twilight, that is, about an hour before the Sun rises or sets. Generally speaking, the further north you are, the lower the Comet will appear in the sky (see opposite).

see its tail peeping over the horizon. As you can see from the diagram, you would get a substantially better view just 10° further south, for then you would be looking at the area shown here below the horizon as well as that above.

As time goes on, it will gradually rise higher in the sky reaching its highest point on about March 26. It is during March and April that the Comet will be at its closest to the Earth, and its tail will be at its longest. Then it will move south, to disappear again. However, *all is still not lost!* It will reappear again in the *evening* sky on about April 20. This time you must look towards the south-east. As April passes, so the Comet will gradually get higher and higher in the sky, with its tail getting shorter and shorter, until by the beginning of May you will be back to using binoculars, and eventually telescopes again. It will be possible to follow it for several more months, but each night it will be further away, with a smaller tail, and ever more difficult to find. Eventually, it will be so far away that even the most powerful telescopes will not be able to find it. Never mind! All that you need to do is sit around for seventy-six years and it will be back again!

When and where to look in the Southern Hemisphere

If you live south of the equator, when the Comet will be visible during the summer months, the best times to see it will be during the first four months of 1986, when it will be visible to the naked eye. If you look in your daily newspaper, near to the weather map, it will tell you the times of sunrise and sunset. The best times to view the Comet are about one-and-a-half hours before sunrise if it is due in the morning or one to one-and-a-half hours after sunset if it is due in the evening. However, you may be lucky enough to actually be able to see it during the daytime on some occasions.

If you live in Northern Australia you will get the first chance to see it. It will appear due west, in the evening sky, during the first few days of January. It will be quite low in the sky so you will need a good vantage point from which to see it. It will disappear below the horizon on about January 15. However, *do not despair*! You will need to change your habits and get up well before sunrise because it will appear again, early in the morning, from about February 24, when it will be visible throughout the Southern Hemisphere. This time you will need to look just south of due east to see it. Now you will really get the best view. Throughout March it will climb higher and higher in the sky, each night appearing a little bit further to the south. It will reach its highest point during the first three days of April, when it will be almost due south. From then on, it will gradually fall back towards the horizon.

However, from April 10 onwards, you will be able to see it both in the morning and in the evening. For evening viewing you will need to look south-east. To begin with, it will again be very low on the horizon, but as time goes on it will climb higher and higher in the sky, this time gradually moving towards the east. By the end of April you will really need binoculars or a telescope in order to see it and, as in the Northern Hemisphere, it will

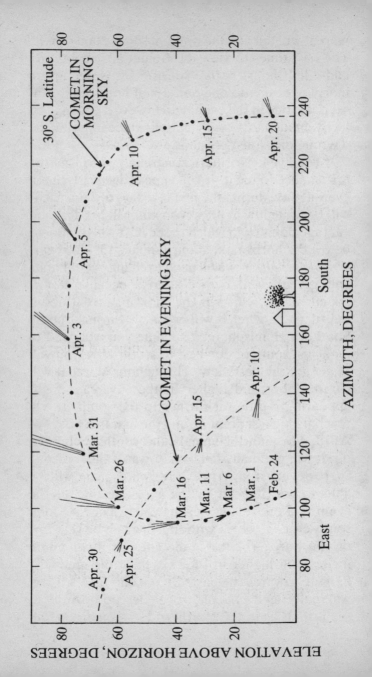

remain just visible for several more months, but each night it will get fainter and its tail will get shorter, making it more difficult to spot until, finally, it will disappear not to be seen again for another seventy-six years.

Where to look for Halley's Comet in the Southern Hemisphere (30° S Latitude) in 1986, when it will be most clearly visible. Comet positions are given for morning astronomical twilight or evening astronomical twilight. Generally speaking, the further south you are, the higher the Comet will appear in the sky (see opposite).

Mega-Teaser 2

Can I take a photograph of the Comet?

(For the answer, turn to page 79.)

3

What is a Comet?

A comet is an object with a star-like nucleus and a
tail pointing away from the Sun which moves in an
elliptical path around the Sun. Because of the long
fiery tail it grows as it approaches the Sun, its
brightness during the night and the fact that it can
on occasions be seen in the daytime, people originally believed that a comet was a 'hot' object, not
unlike the 'shooting stars' that can sometimes be
seen at night. However, it is now known that all of
these original ideas were wrong.

The solid centre of a comet (called the 'nucleus')
is really quite small, ranging from a few hundred
metres to about ten kilometres across. Halley's

Comet is one of the bigger ones. This nucleus is thought to consist of a frozen mixture of water, carbon dioxide, ammonia, possibly methane, molecules of carbon and sulphur, small bits of rock and lots of dust. For most of the time, this is all that you would be able to see of the Comet if you could follow it on its wanderings. It is not until it gets quite close to the Sun, about 450,000,000 kilometres away from it, that it starts to grow its tail.

Distances in the solar system are measured in 'astronomical units'. An astronomical unit, or AU for short, is the average distance between the Earth and the Sun. This works out at about 150,000,000 kilometres (about 93,000,000 miles). So 450,000,000 kilometres is about three AUs.

Although the temperature in space is very low, there is a vast amount of heat, light and other radiations coming from the Sun. If it were not for the Earth's atmosphere we would be burnt to a crisp every time the Sun rose. In space there is no protecting atmosphere and, as a comet gradually gets closer to the Sun, the radiations coming from it gradually cause the surface of the comet to 'sublime'. This means that it changes directly from a frozen solid into a gas. Most things do not sublime. Imagine getting an ice-cube from the refrigerator, putting it into a saucepan and warming it on the cooker. First of all it would melt, forming a liquid, and then it would all boil away, forming a gas – steam. (Don't try this experiment on your own – Mum would be furious if you burnt a hole in one of her saucepans!) In other words, it goes through three stages, changing from solid to liquid, and from liquid to gas. There are, however, some common objects that do sublime. The blocks that you will sometimes find hanging inside lavatories and bathrooms are made of substances that will do this, and the gas that they give off helps to disinfect the room and mask any odours. Ask your Granny about mothballs – they behave in just the same way!

In space there is an effect called the 'solar wind'. You probably know that there is no air in space, so the solar wind is not a wind as we know it on Earth. It is caused by energy moving out from the Sun, and

The structure of the head of Halley's Comet. The size of the coma depends on how close the Comet is to the sun, but it can be many hundreds of thousands of kilometres across

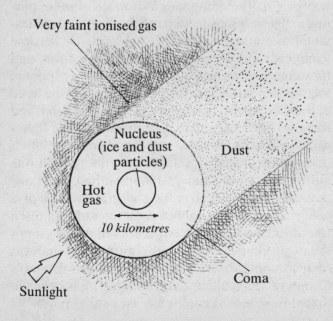

Very faint ionised gas

Nucleus
(ice and dust
particles)

Dust

Hot
gas

10 kilometres

Sunlight

Coma

it has a tremendous effect on our Comet. As the Comet sublimes so particles of dust and molecules of the ice that it is made of are 'blown' off the surface. They spread out around the nucleus of the Comet and fall away behind it. The cloud of dust around the nucleus reflects the sunlight, forming a bright cloud. This is called the 'coma'. There is also a huge cloud of hydrogen gas around the head. This cloud of gas is not visible from Earth, but should be visible to the ultraviolet telescopes on the satellites that are going out to visit Halley's Comet. Together, the nucleus and the coma form the 'head' of the comet.

As the Comet gradually gets nearer to the Sun, it receives more and more ultraviolet radiation. This radiation breaks up the molecules that the Comet was originally made from into much simpler particles. These give off light, as a result of the ultraviolet radiation. Some of the particles become 'charged', changing their electrical nature, and they combine with the solar wind to form a 'plasma tail' or 'ion tail'. The dust that surrounds the head of the Comet also gets blown by the solar wind, and forms a 'dust tail'. This is the 'hair' of the 'hairy star', as the Ancient Greeks called comets.

In fact, comets commonly have more than one tail. A comet was seen in 1903 that had nine tails. Another point worth noting is that the tail of a comet is not necessarily straight; comets are often found with beautiful, flowing, curved tails. Perhaps the most famous comet with a curved tail that was seen in comparatively recent times was Donati's Comet of 1858–1859. Unfortunately, it is believed that this beautiful comet has an orbital period of over 2,000 years, so it is unlikely to be seen again much before the year 4,000.

The question that everyone asks is 'Where do comets come from?' To be quite honest, nobody is very certain, but the most widely accepted theory among astronomers is that there are probably lots of comet-like objects orbiting the Sun, much in the same way as we on Earth do, with all the other planets. However, these orbiting icy rocks are right on the edge of our solar system, far beyond the sight of the most powerful telescopes. Over the millions of years since they were first formed, there must have been some accidents. Perhaps some of them collided and were knocked out of their orbital path, or perhaps they came under the gravitational pull of nearby stars. As a result, their courses were altered. Perhaps some of them were flung off into outer space, never to be seen again. Some of them, however, began to fall towards the gravitational centre of our solar system, the Sun itself.

The orbit of a comet; this may be at any angle to the plane of the solar system

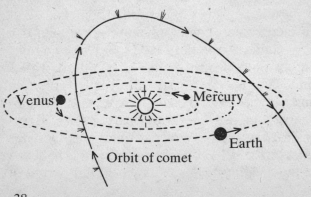

Orbit of comet

Gravity is the attraction that any piece of matter has for other pieces of matter. The bigger the object, the greater the force of gravity that it can exert. Our Sun is the largest mass of material in our solar system, so it exerts the greatest force of gravity. It is our Sun's gravity that keeps us in our orbit around it, and it is the gravity of the Earth that keeps the Moon moving around us. (It also stops creatures that live on Earth floating off into space every time they jump over something!)

As a comet falls towards the Sun, it moves faster and faster through space because of the power of the Sun's gravity. By the time that it gets near to the Sun, it is moving so fast that the combined forces of its own speed and the Sun's gravitational pull whirl it around the Sun and send it shooting off into space again. As it moves away, it gradually slows down,

The way a comet behaves as it reaches its perihelion; the tail always points away from the Sun

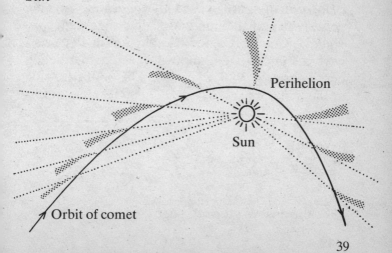

swings around, and then starts to fall towards the Sun again. In its current orbit Halley's Comet reached its furthest point from the Sun in 1948. It is this regular path that comets take that makes it possible to predict how often we are likely to see them, although it takes some very complicated sums to work it out! It is worth remembering that all the time the Comet is under the influence of the solar wind, mentioned earlier, it will fall towards the Sun head first, and go away from the sun tail first.

The orbit of a comet is not like that of a planet. A planet moves in an almost circular path around the Sun, and most of the planets move in roughly the same direction. (In fact, the orbits of planets are slightly squashed circles, with occasional wiggles where one comes close to another planet.) The orbit of a comet is a long, thin shape called an ellipse, with one end of the ellipse near to the Sun, and the other end far out in space. The two most important points for astronomers are the point that is far out in space, called the *aphelion*, and the point that is at the Sun end, called the *perihelion*. Halley's Comet reached its aphelion in 1948, as I have just mentioned, and will reach its perihelion on 9 February 1986, when it will be on the far side of the Sun, and just over 3,200,000,000 kilometres from us.

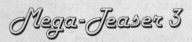

Mega-Teaser 3

Do comets ever wear out?
(For the answer, turn to page 79.)

4

Who was Halley?

In order to understand who Edmond Halley was, and why he was so important in his day, it is necessary to look back many thousands of years, and to see why an astronomer – a person who studies the stars, planets and other heavenly bodies – was an important person in most societies.

In the early days, man would sit outside his cave or wooden hut and look into the sky and imagine that he could see pictures in the patterns that appeared night after night, and year after year. After a while, he noticed that certain patterns appeared in the sky at certain times of the year, and that certain 'stars' seemed to appear at times that were out of step with the other stars. (We now know that these are the planets that are part of our solar system.) After a while, he would probably be able to predict eclipses of the Sun and the Moon. But before this and of primary importance were the predictions he was able to make about the pattern of the year – the seasons. In particular, estimating the right time of year for planting and harvesting was crucial to the survival of man. And this gave stature to the first astronomers. As nearly every primitive region equated events in heaven with those on Earth so the priests would point out the connection between certain regular patterns in the skies and events on Earth. This led in time to interest in astrology – a superstition predicting future events from the study of the sky.

As time passed, the importance of the astrologer diminished and that of the astronomer increased. (The difference between the two is important – neither likes to be confused with the other.) Edmond Halley was an astronomer. He was one of the increasing band of scientists who hoped to find out about how the world had begun, what the importance is of our Sun and our position in the Galaxy, and to discover the answers to lots of other difficult questions. Today's scientists are still seeking answers, sending unmanned space vehicles off on journeys that will last for many, many years. Of course, Edmond Halley did not have all the advantages of a modern scientist. He had to rely on his own eyes, on telescopes that were very limited compared with even the cheapest of modern instruments, and on the notes and stories that had been passed down from father to son over many generations. These notes were often inaccurate, and frequently had more than a little of the fairy story about them. What Halley achieved with his limited resources – it was much more than just the prediction of the Comet that is now named after him – is quite incredible. Think how much more *you* could manage!

Edmond Halley (1656–1742)

Halley was born in Haggerston, in the parish of St Leonards, Shoreditch, east London in the autumn of 1656. He came from quite a rich family. His father was a soap manufacturer who had originally come from Derbyshire, and Edmond was one of two sons, but the other died in his youth. He also had a sister who died in infancy. He was sent to St Paul's School in London and proved a clever pupil; he studied well in mathematics and classics, and was made Captain of the school when he was fifteen. Already he was most interested in the Earth and the stars, and he had made such a close study of the heavens that a man named Moxon, who made globes of the Earth for his living, said of Edmond, 'If one star was moved in the sky, he would be the first to find it out!'

Edmond was only sixteen when he went to Queen's College, Oxford. His arrival must have caused considerable interest, because he brought with him a telescope that was about seven metres long. He set this up near to his lodgings in the university, and made several important observations while he was there. These included a lunar eclipse in 1675, and a large sunspot in August 1676. At about the same time he saw the 'occultation' of Mars by the Moon; this is when the Moon passes directly between us and the planet Mars. Apart from being an extremely good observer he was also an excellent mathematician, and just before he was twenty years old he sent to the Royal Society – the most important scientific organisation in England – a written paper that he called 'A Direct and Geometrical Method of finding the Aphelia and Eccentricity of the Planets'. (See the *Glossary of Terms Used* on page 82 for the meanings of these words.)

Throughout his university life he continued his observations, inventing a new method for predicting solar eclipses, and noting movements in the orbits of Jupiter and Saturn. He realised that if he were to *prove* that these orbits had not hitherto been correctly ascertained he would need to find out a great deal more about the stars seen in the southern half of the globe. In November 1676 he left the university before he got his degree, and with an allowance of £300 from his father set sail for the island of St Helena in the south Atlantic ocean off the west coast of Africa. He was helped in his travel by a letter from King Charles II to the great trading concern called the East India Company, who provided him with transport.

Edmond spent one-and-a-half years in St Helena, and in that time he was able to fix the positions of 341 stars. He found this small number very disappointing, but he had not allowed for the clouds and mists that covered the island for much of the time. However, his work did lay down the foundations for the astronomy of the Southern Hemisphere. On his return he presented to the King a catalogue and plane map of the stars that could be seen in the south, and as a reward for his work he was presented with a Master of Arts degree at Oxford in 1678.

Edmond continued his observations of the stars and the planets throughout his life, but his work involved much more than just this. He was elected to the Royal Society when he was only twenty-two years old, and was for many years its secretary. His other work included a survey of the currents in the English Channel; a study on how the magnetic compass varied in different parts of the globe – very important work at that time, as explorers and traders relied on the compass to find their way around the Earth; studies on trade winds and monsoons, and how the waters of the seas circulated through the action of Sun and winds.

Halley married in 1682 when he was twenty-six, and had several children, although some of them died when they were still young. His own father died when he was twenty-eight, and Edmond found that he was no longer as well off as he had thought. In spite of this, he was most helpful in enabling his friend, the great mathematician Isaac Newton, to publish his famous book the *Philosophiae naturalis principia mathematica*, in which he first told the world about his theory of gravity. Edmond had already realised that the theory of gravity helped explain many of his own theories, which may be why he was so interested in it. He was made Astronomer Royal in 1720.

The position of Astronomer Royal had been created in the year 1675, when the Royal Observatory at Greenwich was built. King Charles II, who had an interest in many branches of science appointed the Reverend John Flamsteed 'our astronomical observator', at a salary of £100 a year. His instructions were that he should study the stars and planets, and keep the King informed of any new developments or exciting discoveries. Flamsteed held the appointment until his death in 1719, and Edmond Halley took over the post the following year, which gave him the opportunity to continue with his observations, particularly those of the Moon.

His most famous book was *Astronomiae Cometicae Synopsis*, published in 1705, in which he published the orbits of twenty-four comets he had studied. He predicted the return of a particularly bright comet in 1758, appealing to the world to remember that its orbit 'was first discovered by an Englishman'. Unfortunately, Edmond never lived to see it. He became paralysed in his right arm in 1736, the year in which his wife died, and for the next few years gradually became more and more ill, although his brain was still as acute as ever. Finally, being tired of drinking the cordials that doctors prescribed for him, he asked for a glass of wine, drank it and died, on 14 January 1742 at the age of eighty-five. He is buried next to his wife in the churchyard at Lee, near Greenwich. His tomb is marked by a stone erected the following year by his two daughters.

Edmond Halley was a remarkable man. During his life he was considered to be the most prominent astronomer in Britain, and only Isaac Newton surpassed him as a scientist and mathematician. To look at, he was about 1.75 metres (roughly five feet, nine inches) in height, thin, with fair hair. He always spoke in a lively and entertaining manner, which made him a very popular person in the society of his time. He was respected among scientists for being able to combine his great knowledge and perception with a generous and honest disposition, and was known as always being fair and considerate in his dealings with those around him. He was well known among kings and princes, and his portrait was painted by many of the famous artists of his age. It is only fitting that his name should be recalled every seventy-six years or so, because he was one of the truly great men of English science.

Mega-Teaser 4

Who is the current Astronomer Royal in England?
(For the answer, turn to page 80.)

5

Early Sightings of the Comet

As we saw earlier, Edmond Halley was not the first person to see the Comet that is now named after him. It had, in fact, been seen many times before, and in history many references had been made to it, and many legends built up around its appearance. What Edmond Halley did was to work out, by a lot of research into old documents and stories, that the Comet that was named after him was one that had been seen on previous occasions, and that its orbit had a definite period when it could be seen from the Earth in all its glory. He had, in fact, charted and predicted the appearance of many comets, but this one is the most important, being one of the brightest and most spectacular, and the one that nearly everyone gets at least one chance to see.

One of the first pictures of Halley's Comet: the 684 AD visit as recorded in the Nuremberg Chronicles

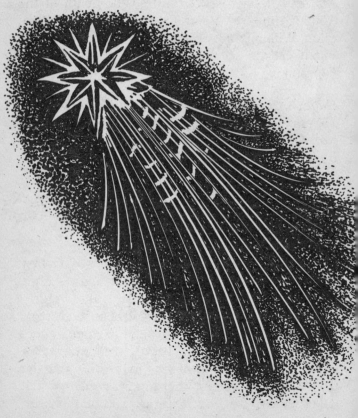

The comet that we now call Halley's Comet was first recorded in the year 240 BC by the Chinese. Its return has been recorded on each occasion, somewhere on Earth, every time it has visited us.

It has always been considered, along with most other comets, to be a sign of bad fortune, and indeed many famous events have occurred around the times that the Comet has appeared: Jerusalem fell to the Romans following a siege four years after its appearance in AD 66 and, when it appeared in AD 455, it supposedly foretold the death of the Roman Emperor Valerian. It appeared in 1066, when William the Conqueror invaded England, and it can be seen embroidered on the Bayeux Tapestry.

Halley's Comet as it appears on the Bayeux Tapestry – a good sign for King William of Normandy, but not so good for King Harold of England!

Halley's Comet was considered to be such an evil object when it appeared in 1456 that Pope Calixtus III excommunicated it from the Roman Catholic Church, claiming that it was an 'agent of the devil'! In 1668, Stanislav Lubeinietski wrote with some irony '. . . Never had there been a disaster without a comet, or a comet without a disaster. Had there not been a comet overhead which had been responsible for the epidemic of sneezing sickness amongst the cats of the Rhenish areas of Westphalia?'

People have always been fascinated by comets, and for a long time they were considered simply to be weird or unlucky objects that appeared inside the atmosphere of the Earth itself. It was not until the great sixteenth-century Danish astronomer, Tycho Brahe, made a detailed study of the Great Comet that appeared in the year 1577 that some of the mystery surrounding comets began to disappear, and it was realised that they were truly members of our solar system. Even so, when Halley's Comet appeared in 1910 there was considerable panic among some people. Scientists had predicted that the Earth would pass through the tail of the Comet, and people imagined that mankind would be stricken with poisonous gas. In fact, there probably are very small quantities of the gas cyanogen in the tail of the Comet, but it is far too small an amount to cause any damage to people on Earth, even if we did pass through the Comet's tail. Several unscrupulous people made a great deal of money from selling gas masks and 'comet pills', guaranteed to make you safe from its supposedly evil effects. There was even a story – probably an invention – about an attempt at a human sacrifice, not in some primitive country, but in Oklahoma, America.

However, not all people thought that comets were evil. In earlier times the painting of the Nativity by Giotto di Bondone used Halley's Comet to represent the Star of Bethlehem, and the Nativity is considered to be an event of great joy and hope for mankind. Comets are mentioned in the Bible, and by St Thomas Aquinas in his religious work, *Summa Theologica*.

Even nowadays, comets do raise peculiar questions. In 1978 the two astronomers Hoyle and Wickramasinghe suggested that comets could possibly carry with them germs that were unknown to man, and they suggested that outbreaks of influenza in some schools in Britain might be as a result of particles coming from comets. It is an interesting idea, and helps to underline the fact that with all our modern equipment we still do not know enough about these unusual heavenly bodies.

Mega-Teaser 5

Might there be other comets waiting to be discovered that no one has yet seen?

(For the answer, turn to page 80.)

6

Things that go Whizz in the Night

To look up into the night-time sky is, at first, very confusing indeed. There seem to be so many points of light, and they all appear to be of different sizes, colours and brightness, so that to attempt to pick out just one of them, or even a group of them, looks almost impossible. However, there is a system that you can follow to work out just what you are looking at. We will explain it by working outwards from the Earth, into deep space.

The two most obvious objects in the sky are our Sun, which is seen during the day, and the Moon, which is seen at night, and sometimes also during the day. The Sun is a star. It is so near to us, and so bright, that when it is visible it is not usually possible to see much else. Our Earth, along with a number of other planets, is in orbit around the Sun. The Sun is our source of energy, which comes from a nuclear reaction taking place inside it. Should the Sun 'go out', our Earth would very quickly become an uninhabitable, extremely cold lump of rock, even though there is still some heat in the core of the Earth. It would no longer be able to support life. Fortunately for us, this is most unlikely to happen! The Sun's mass is very big compared with that of the Earth, being 332,958 times the size of our planet. However, as stars go, by no means has it the largest mass.

The Moon is our satellite. It is in an orbit around us, much as we are in an orbit around the Sun. Although the Moon looks almost as big as the Sun, its diameter is in fact only about one-quarter the size of the Earth's. Gravity is only one-sixth that of the Earth so if you weigh thirty kilograms on Earth, you will only weigh five on the Moon. You could jump six times as high as you do now, and throw a ball six times as far. Unfortunately, life on the Moon would present a number of problems. Because there is no atmosphere, you would need to live permanently in a space suit. The parts of the Moon that are facing the Sun are extremely hot – hotter than boiling water – and those parts that face away from the Sun are colder than our coldest nights anywhere on Earth, being more than 167 degrees Celsius below freezing point.

One interesting thing about the Moon is that it

turns around once every time it makes an orbit of the Earth. That is why everyone on Earth sees the same 'face' of the Moon, no matter where they live. The moon is not a hot object as our Sun is. The only times that we can see it are when it is in a position where the light from the Sun can bounce off its surface and reflect back to Earth. Our Moon is not the only one that exists. Many planets have moons, and some have more than one. The Earth and Pluto each have one; Mars and Neptune have two each; Uranus has five; Jupiter has sixteen and Saturn has more than twenty. Mercury and Venus have no moons at all.

Our planet is one of a number that are circling around the Sun. The Sun, with its group of planets and their moons, is called the solar system. We can often see the other members of our solar system in the sky as they travel on their orbits around the Sun. All the planets in our solar system travel around the Sun in approximately the same plane, so sometimes they are on the same side of the Sun as us, and sometimes they are on the other side. When they are on the other side they are too difficult to see, so we can only really see them at night. The planets are so much nearer than the stars and they usually give out a steady clear light, being less likely to twinkle than stars.

Some planets are easy to recognise. Mars, which is close to us, usually appears slightly red, and was for many years known as the 'Red Planet'. If you have a powerful pair of binoculars or a good telescope you can sometimes see the rings around Saturn. But more readily identifiable is Jupiter, with its four large satellites. The other planets are not as easy to recognise, and you would need to look at a star chart for the right time of year to spot them with any certainty.

Taking the planets in order according to their present distance from the Sun, Mercury comes first, and its orbit is the quickest, taking only eighty-eight days, compared with the Earth's 365. If you lived on Mercury, you would have a birthday every eighty-eight days! Venus comes next. This is the hottest of the planets, and is our nearest neighbour after the Moon. It is also the brightest of our planets that you are likely to see, being only 41,360,000 kilometres away when it is at its closest point. It is Venus that appears in the western sky as the 'evening star'. Earth comes after Venus, and it is probably the most beautiful of the planets when seen from space, with its shining blue and green colouring. Then comes Mars, on the other side of us. Because it has ice-caps on each of its poles, and peculiar markings on its surface, and because it changes colour throughout its year, people thought for a long time that other beings might live on Mars, and stories about 'Martian invaders' were always being written. Nowadays, people believe that if there is any life there at all, it is only likely to be a very simple kind of plant life, at most, bacteria. The Viking space mission of 1976 showed no signs of life.

Next comes Jupiter. It is the biggest of the planets, being more than 317 times as big as the Earth. It also has the shortest day, spinning around on its axis once every nine hours and fifty minutes, compared with our twenty-four. Jupiter is most famous for its great 'red spot', which is apparently caused by a group of red-coloured clouds in its atmosphere. Saturn comes next, and is famous for the rings around it. These rings are believed to be made up of innumerable pieces of icy dust and small rocks, all orbiting the planet like small moons. The rings are not always visible from Earth, because they disappear when viewed from the side. Saturn seems to be made of the lightest material of any of the planets. (The Earth seems to be made of the heaviest material.) Uranus comes next, then Pluto – at least until about 1999 – and lastly, Neptune. On average, Pluto is the farthest from the Sun as the following diagram shows. But its orbit occasionally brings it in nearer than Neptune as is the case at the moment.

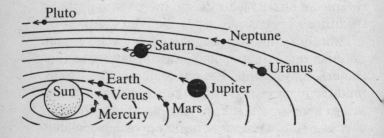

The Sun and planets that make up our solar system

Because all the planets are travelling around the Sun at different speeds, it is most unusual for them to arrange themselves in a straight line.

The other most obvious things that you will see in the night sky are the stars, and at first glance it seems impossible to make any sense of them at all. There are so many everywhere that you look that it seems totally confusing. However, if you make an effort you can make some sense of them. Before you try, there are some things that you must remember. If we take all the stars that there are, we call it the Galaxy. This Galaxy actually has a shape. It is like a flying saucer, a huge disc, thick in the middle and thinner at the edges. We are close to the edge, and if we look across towards the centre of the disc we see the incredible band of stars called the Milky Way. To us on Earth the stars all seem to be the same distance away. But they are not, and this partly explains why some stars seem to be brighter than others. All stars are in some way like our Sun. In other words, they are great glowing masses of material giving out energy in the form of light, heat and various other radiations. They may or may not have planets – we are so far away that it is difficult to tell.

Another point to remember is that stars are not all the same size. Some are much bigger than others, and some are much brighter than others, and the biggest stars are not necessarily the brightest or the nearest. In fact our nearest star, Proxima Centauri, is so faint that it is hardly visible at all to the naked eye. Sometimes a star explodes, and forms a supernova, an extremely bright light that eventually fades. These often leave behind 'nebulae', clouds of luminous gases that often look like very fine cloth. One of the most famous nebulae is called the Veil Nebula for this reason.

To help us find our way about the sky, we group the stars together into constellations. I am sure that in the summer you have sat outside watching clouds go by, and found pictures in their shapes. So, in the past, people looked at the stars and thought that they could see shapes up there. Of course, since this was a long time ago, they gave these constellations names of objects that they were likely to see in their everyday life, such as 'bear' (Ursa), 'archer' (Sagittarius) and 'lion' (Leo). We still use these shapes to find our way around the sky, and still call many constellations by their ancient names.

You must remember that although the stars in a constellation may seem to be close together, in fact they can be enormous distances apart. We measure the distances between stars in light years. A beam of light moves forward at a speed of 299,792 kilometres (186,281 miles) a second. Imagine how far it would travel in a whole year! For those of you who want to work it out, multiply 299,792 by the number of seconds in a minute, that answer by the number of minutes in an hour, that answer by the number of hours in a day, and that answer by the number of days in a year. You will probably need quite a large piece of paper for your sum!

All the objects that I have mentioned so far have regular patterns of movement, or fixed positions in the sky. There are, however, some objects that do not have regular patterns of movement, and that move so quickly that sometimes you only see them out of the corner of your eye. These are some of the huge number of bits of rock and dust that are floating around in space. Normally, we cannot see them at all, but if they wander too close to the

The path of Halley's Comet on the Celestial Sphere during November 1985–May 1986 (see opposite)

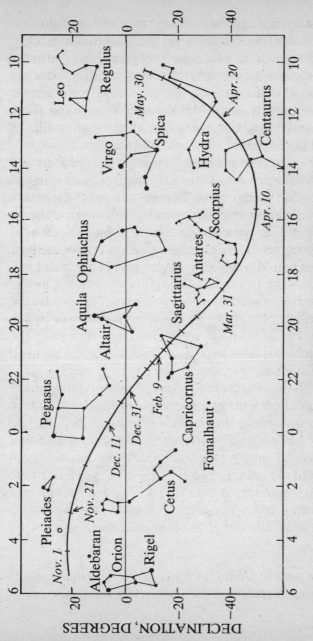

Earth, they get caught by our gravitational pull, and begin to fall towards us. They fall faster and faster, until they hit our atmosphere, by which time they are going so fast that they begin to burn up, and all that you see is a streak of light that moves very quickly across the sky and disappears. These shooting stars, or meteors as they are properly called, are quite common, and sometimes you may see several in a night.

Most meteoroids are very small particles indeed, and they burn up long before they get to the Earth. Very rarely, however, some of them do manage to get all the way through the atmosphere, and actually fall to the ground. Usually they do not do much damage, although this is not always the case.

Meteoroids that actually manage to fall to Earth are called meteorites. Most countries have sites where meteorites have struck the Earth. Some of these sites are very large indeed and are tourist attractions, but most are only of local interest. See if you can find out where your nearest 'meteorite strike' took place! If you ever see an actual meteorite falling you will be very lucky indeed!

Mega-Teaser 6

What is a Black Hole?
(For the answer, turn to page 80.)

7

Things to look out for

Although this book is mostly about Halley's Comet, I hope that it will give you some idea of the many other fascinating things that can be seen in the sky at night. A comet is an interesting object, but it is only one of the hundreds of subjects that are worth a really close look.

Comets are really divided into two groups – those which we all get excited about and those we don't really notice! Of these, most common are the latter. In fact, you may be surprised to know that six or seven minor comets pass the Earth each year! Most of them, unfortunately, are much too small to be seen by the naked eye, although you may be able to pick them out with a good telescope. Often they do not develop tails, which makes them even more difficult to see.

Comets are usually named after the first person to see them, although some, like Halley's Comet, are named after the first person to work out their orbits. There is always the possibility that you may score a first, in which case your name would go down in history as the discoverer of a comet! One of the reasons for this is that the time that a comet takes to complete its period, or orbit, can vary from as little as three years up to several thousand years. In other words, there are probably comets coming towards us that are not yet known to anyone! A great comet appeared a few years ago, and was named after the person who was the first to spot it – an astronomer by the name of Kohoutek. This has now disappeared into space again, and is not expected back for several thousand years. I have given a list of notable comets and their periods below.

Notable Comets

Comet	Period	Comet	Period
Encke	3.3	Comas à Sola	8.9
Grigg-Skjellerup	5.1	Väisäla	10.9
Pons-Winnecke	6.4	Tuttle	13.7
Kopff	6.4	Crommelin	27.9
Giacobini-Zinner	6.5	Stephan-Oterma	37.7
D'Arrest	6.4	Westphal	61.7
Borelly	6.8	Brorsen-Metcalf	61.9
Faye	7.4	Olbers	69.6
Whipple	7.4	Pons-Brooks	70.9
Schaumasse	8.2	Halley	76.1

Another fascinating group of objects to watch for are meteors. Again, these are divided into two groups. One group is predictable; in other words we can say to a greater or lesser extent when we are likely to see them. These meteors come in bunches, and travel through space in straight lines, intercepting the Earth in its orbit. They are believed to originate from comets in many cases, because the times that we see them match the times that in past years we have seen comets. Others are thought to be pieces of asteroids (minor planets).

These groups of meteors can sometimes produce amazing displays, because so many of them can appear together in a very short time. From Earth it may appear as if they are all falling in different directions. This is a trick of perspective, caused by the fact that we are standing still on the Earth, and the meteors are moving towards us. The meteor paths really follow parallel lines, and can be compared with, for example, railway lines. Imagine that you are standing on a bridge overlooking a railway line. The railway has a fence either side and there is a power line running alongside the railway and over your head. All these straight lines – the railway, the fences, and the power cables – seem to disappear at a point on the horizon even though they follow parallel paths. However, when meteors hit the Earth all that we see is the very short piece of their 'line' as they burn up in our atmosphere. This is why they may appear to be going in all directions.

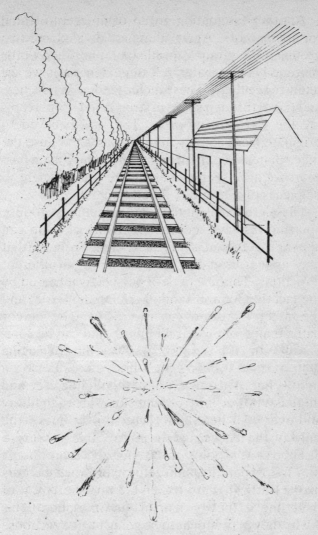

A trick of perspective: the meteor paths really follow parallel lines and can be compared with railway lines which seem to radiate from a small point in the distance

Below I have given a list of the six most usual meteor showers, and the approximate dates when they may be seen. You will notice that some of the dates co-incide with the time that you will be 'comet-spotting', so now you have two things to look for!

Notable Meteor Showers

Name	Date
Quadrantids	4 January
Lyrids	19–24 April
Perseids	1–17 August
Orionids	15–25 October
Leonids	14–17 November
Geminids	9–13 December

The other class of meteors consists of those that are just rocks wandering about in space. These are called 'sporadic' meteors, and will suddenly and totally unexpectedly appear. However, they are still well worth looking for, and several are seen on most nights of the year.

The unexpected is always worth noting. Some years ago I saw a small, faint light moving slowly across the sky. It was not an aeroplane, nor a star. It was much too fast to be a comet, and too slow to be a meteor. I rather hoped that it would be a rocket full of little green men! However, when I telephoned the British Astronomical Association, they were able to tell me that it was a section from an American rocket that had been launched some weeks before, and was now just beginning to fall back towards the Earth. I was able to see it because the Sun was just below the horizon, and the light was reflecting off the gleaming polished skin of the rocket. Eventually, it fell into the atmosphere over India, and burnt up just like a meteor would. There is an amazing amount of 'space junk' floating around our planet these days, and much of it will eventually fall back down again. Don't worry about getting bonked on the head; it will burn up long before it reaches you!

Mega-Teaser 7

What is the most unusual object that I am likely to see in space?

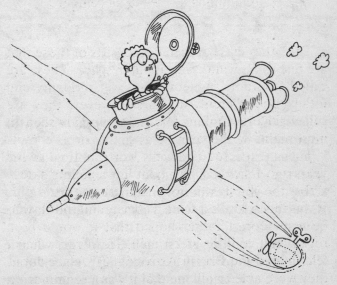

(For the answer, turn to page 81.)

8

How to start Studying Astronomy

One of the best points about astronomy is that the equipment needed can be as simple or as complicated as you care to make it. You can, if you wish, spend a great deal of money on a reflector telescope, or you can perform equally interesting but rather less detailed work with nothing more than your own eyes.

If, while looking at Halley's Comet, you decide that you want to study astronomy in greater detail, you must organise yourself in a proper and scientific manner. The first items of equipment that you will need are a notebook and something to write with! It is very foolish to try to rely on your memory, as you are certain to make mistakes. It is far better to have a written record, especially if it is a record that is made on the spot. This is why the notebook is essential. In this you will need to make the following observations: Firstly, you should make a note of the date and time, preferably using the 24-hour clock to avoid confusion. Let us suppose that you saw a very bright star at twelve o'clock on Christmas Day, 1985, just before your Christmas dinner. (This has been done before, as you may have heard!) You would record the time and the date as follows:

Year	Month	Day	Time
1985	December	25	1200

The next recording you will need to make should state what it was that you were observing. This should form the next column after your date and time. Now you have the problem of identifying exactly whereabouts in the sky you first saw the object that you are making a note of. There are two ways of doing this. The most obvious way is to give a direction; for example, this could either be a compass point, such as south-east, or a compass bearing. Compass bearings start at due north, and move around in a circle through east, south and west, finally arriving back at north. They travel through 360 degrees, so north is 0 (or 360) degrees, east is 90 degrees, south is 180 degrees and west is 270 degrees. South-east, then, would be 135 degrees.

You must follow your direction with an 'elevation', that is how high in the sky the object was when you spotted it. This is done by dividing the quarter-circle between the horizon and the zenith (the point directly over your head) into 90 degrees, the same as with your direction finding. All that you now need to do is to work out how many degrees above the horizon the object was when you saw it. You can do this with a protractor, which you can buy at most stationers, but it is just as easy to make your own portable device though probably it is best if you ask an adult to help you to do this.

You will need a piece of plywood or hardboard about thirty centimetres square, a tube about one centimetre in diameter and thirty centimetres in length, some quick-setting glue, a bolt with two nuts, and a pointer made from a straight piece of wire that you can bend into a loop at one end. Draw onto the wood a 'quadrant', or quarter of a circle. Mark around the edge of the circle the degrees from 0 to 90 – you do not need to mark every degree – once every five or ten degrees should be accurate enough. You will need to ask an adult to drill a hole through the corner of your quadrant where the two straight lines meet. With the bolt and nuts, hang the wire next to your scale, making sure that it can swing freely. Now glue the tube on top of one of the straight edges, so that when the tube is 'horizontal', or pointing straight out in front of you, the pointer rests at 0 degrees, and when the tube is pointing 'vertically', or straight up in the air, the pointer reads 90 degrees. You need to hold the quadrant so that the 90 degree mark is nearest to you. If you now look through the tube at an object in the air, your pointer should swing round, and indicate how many degrees above the horizon the object is.

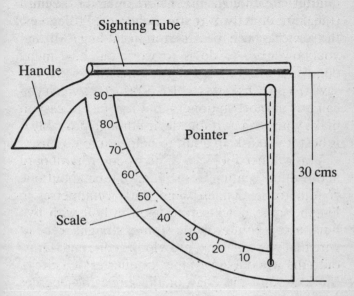

A clinometer

If you are lucky enough to have an astronomical telescope, you may well find that the bearings that you need to record are marked on the stand and on the side of the telescope. In this case, you must make sure that you erect your telescope so that it is quite level on the ground, and so that the bearing marked 0 or 360 degrees points towards the north.

The other, and in some respects easier, way of indicating where you first see something is to identify the constellation that it was in when you saw it. This is all right if you really do know your constellations, but they do take a little time to learn. As the year passes, different stars and constellations appear, so the season will have a bearing on observations. Although the above method is much quicker, it is not really accurate. Professional astronomers use the first method.

The last column on your page should be reserved for any notes that you may care to make. These should include such details as colour, if it is a meteor or planet that you are looking at, details of any movement in the case of meteors, brightness in the case of stars, and really anything else that you think is of interest. It is as well to make this quite a big column!

There are two other essential pieces of equipment: one is a plastic bag that you can put your notebook into should it threaten to rain – it would be a great shame if hours of careful note-making were ruined by a sudden shower – and the second is a couple of elastic bands to hold the pages down in case it gets windy.

Apart from your notebook, a pair of binoculars is very useful. You will need a compass for your bearings, and an elevation-meter or clinometer. You should always dress up warmly; it is easy to take clothes off if you get too hot, but difficult to put more on if you are a long way from home. A strong thermos flask, filled with something to keep you warm (make sure Dad does not fill it with whisky, if he decides to come with you!), some sandwiches, a small folding stool to sit on, and a board to rest your notebook on, and you are ready. Try not to forget your pencil!

Of course, it is always more fun to do things with other people who share your interests. Many towns have amateur astronomical societies, and you can find out where these are either by looking in a telephone directory such as the Yellow Pages or by asking at your local library. If neither of these works, write to your national astronomical association (Junior Branch), some addresses for which are given at the end of this book (along with other useful addresses and interesting places to visit). Of course, you could always form your own club at school, although obviously it is best if you can find an adult who will help you to organise things. Science teachers are often willing to help, and will probably be able to put you in touch with someone who is interested in what you are doing, even if they cannot help directly themselves. Again, your national astronomical association will probably be pleased to help you in any way that they can. They are often particularly interested in hearing about sightings of meteors.

It is obviously best to study astronomy in the darkest place you can, away from street lights and the smoke and dust of cities and towns. However, many people live in areas where it is difficult to find a place from which to observe the stars and planets. This does not mean that you should give up any attempt to observe them. Many useful observations can be made from bedroom windows and back gardens, which have the advantage of having fixed points, such as television aerials and chimneys, against which you can measure the movement of the stars and planets. It is also easy to make your observations at any convenient time, without the need for long preparations for a lengthy expedition.

I hope this book will encourage many of you to become amateur astronomers. Much valuable work is performed each year by amateurs, and Britain's most famous astronomer, Patrick Moore, started off in just the same way as I have suggested that you start. Happy star-gazing!

Mega-Teaser 8

Could I build my own telescope?
(For the answer, turn to page 81.)

Answers to the Mega-Teasers

1. *What would happen if we should get too close to the Comet, or even if it should hit our planet?*
I must answer this in two parts. To begin with, it is unlikely that Halley's Comet will ever hit us. However, we have got quite close to it on a number of occasions, and it is believed that in 1910 we actually passed through the tail of the Comet. Although there were more meteors than usual seen at that time, there were no other ill effects. Although the Comet's tail looks quite solid from the Earth, it is in reality very, very thin. There is about one tiny particle of dust in an area of space about the size of a large room. So, in this case, there is nothing to worry about!

Just after midnight on the 30 June 1908, in a part of Siberia, Russia, there was an enormous explosion. It devastated an area of about 3,750 square kilometres, with trees being laid flat in lines pointing out from the centre of the explosion. The shock of the explosion was felt as much as 1,000 kilometres away. Many people believe that this was the result of a collision between the Earth and a comet, particularly because not many traces of meteorite particles have been found. Fortunately, this explosion occured in an area where no one lived, so as far as anyone could tell nobody was hurt.

If this was indeed a comet, then it is obvious that if such a collision happened again, especially if the point of impact was in an area where a great number of people lived, then it would indeed be a disaster of epic size. However, the probability of its happening is very remote indeed.

2. *Can I take a photograph of the Comet?*

Yes, you can, provided that your camera is fitted with a shutter lock (denoted by a 'B' on the shutter speed settings). You will need to open the lens as wide as possible (use the lowest 'f' setting), and use a fast film (one with a high ASA/DIN number). You will need to put the camera on a very steady tripod, or clamp it in some way so that it is absolutely still. Use a cable-release to release the shutter, and then you will have to experiment! Try your first exposure at about ten seconds, and gradually build up to about ten minutes. On the longer exposures you will be able to see 'star trails', caused by the rotation of the Earth. You can use colour film for prints or transparencies, or black and white film.

3. *Do comets ever wear out?*

Yes, they do. One of our most regular comets, Encke's Comet, which returns every three years and four months, is gradually getting fainter, and some people expect it to have disappeared altogether by the year 1994. However, this might be disputed by many scientists.

Every time a comet moves round the Sun, it loses about a metre from its surface. Obviously this means that each time a comet returns, it gets a little smaller, and will eventually fade away to nothing. It will be many thousands of years before Halley's Comet becomes too small to see.

One comet that was observed regularly in the 1800s was seen one year to have split into two pieces. As the years passed, so the two parts became increasingly fainter, and finally faded from sight. Nowadays we often get a meteor shower that comes at the same time as this comet would have been due.

4. *Who is the current Astronomer Royal in England?*
The current Astronomer Royal is Professor F. Graham Smith, Director of Jodrell Bank. The post is an honorary one conferred by the Queen, and most Astronomers Royal have been Directors of the Royal Observatory.

5. *Might there be other comets waiting to be discovered that no one has yet seen?*
Yes! See Chapter 7.

6. *What is a Black Hole?*
It is believed that when a really massive star collapses, its field of gravity is so great that nothing, not even light or radiation, can escape from it. This stage is commonly known as a Black Hole.

7. What is the most unusual object that I am likely to see in space?

This is a very difficult question to answer, because nobody can predict what is to be found next in the vastness of space. You may be lucky enough to be one of the few people observing when there is a spectacular meteor shower. You may even discover a new comet! However, I think that one of the most exciting sights to see must be a supernova, a large star that suddenly explodes, flooding its corner of the heavens with light. A supernova is totally unpredictable, and you have just as much chance of detecting one with a pair of binoculars as with the most expensive radio-telescope on Earth!

8. Could I build my own telescope?

The answer to this question is 'Yes, certainly, but you will need a little help'. I have seen very good telescopes made from such items as lengths of plastic drainpipe, which were as effective as telescopes costing several hundred pounds. However, you must bear in mind these facts. You will have to buy lenses or mirrors, depending on what type of telescope you intend to make. You cannot make them yourself, and they will cost quite a lot of money. Secondly, a great deal of precision is needed in distancing and securing the lenses. Thirdly, it would be helpful to have some understanding of light refraction and reflection.

It may be a particularly worthwhile project to attempt at school. It is beyond the scope of this book to tell you how to make a telescope but your local library will almost certainly have, or be able to get for you, books that can tell you how it can be done.

Glossary of Terms Used

Altitude: Angle of elevation above the horizon.

Aphelion: The point in the orbit of a planet or a comet when it is at its greatest distance from the Sun. (See also perihelion.)

Astrologer: A person who studies the stars and

planets because he or she believes that they affect people's lives. Not to be confused with the next person on the list!

Astronomer: A person who makes a scientific study of the heavenly bodies.

Atmosphere: The belt of mixed gases that surrounds the Earth, and many other planets. In our case, it is a mixture of nitrogen (74%), oxygen (23%), carbon dioxide, water vapour and a number of other gases. In the case of the Earth these gases form a belt that is about ninety-five kilometres thick which helps to protect us from the effects of ultraviolet rays. The atmosphere also helps to maintain the temperature throughout the world within certain levels. However, one of its effects is that it 'bends' and scatters the light from any object in space, and confuses the picture.

AU: (Astronomical unit) A convenient measure of distances in near space. One AU is the average distance of the Earth from the Sun, and works out to be just under 150,000,000 kilometres. It is generally used to measure distances inside our own solar system as it is a comparatively 'short' distance in astronomical terms.

Azimuth: An angle (usually) measured around the horizon from North through East.

Coma: The bright haze that spreads around the nucleus of a comet. It is caused by dust particles being blown off the comet as it sublimes. The coma, with the nucleus, forms the head of the comet.

Constellation: A group of stars that appear to be close together in the sky, and which appear to make a shape or picture. It is useful to be able to recognise some constellations, as they will help you find your way around the sky.

Eccentricity: Any deviation in the orbit of a planet from the true circle. The orbits of all comets are eccentric, as the paths that they travel are ellipses.

Eclipse: Something that happens when two heavenly bodies line up in the sky with one in front of the other. A solar eclipse can either be a full eclipse, when the Moon completely covers the Sun, or a partial eclipse, when the Moon only covers a part of the Sun; they usually last for only a few minutes. You must take care when looking at eclipses to make sure that you do not damage your eyes by staring directly at the Sun.

Ellipse: The shape, like a squashed circle or the outline of a rugby ball, that is the path taken by a comet as it travels through space. Most orbits are elliptical to some extent, but they are rarely as squashed as the orbit of a comet.

Galaxy: A group of stars that is visible as a patch of light without its being possible to pick out each star separately.

Gravity: The force of attraction that any body

exerts on any other body that comes near to it. The more massive the object, the greater the force that it produces. It is gravity that keeps us on the Earth, that keeps the Moon revolving around the Earth and keeps the Earth and its Moon revolving around the Sun.

Horizon: That line where the sky appears to meet the Earth. It is difficult to define exactly, because the horizon that you see from the bottom of a hill is a different shape, and a lot nearer, than the horizon that you will see from the top of a hill. It is used, in conjunction with the zenith, the azimuth and the altitude to define exactly where to look for a particular object in the sky.

Infrared: A form of light that is not visible to human eyes, although it can be seen by some animals. Our eyes pick up light from a range of different colours, starting with red, orange, yellow, blue, green, indigo and ending with violet. Infrared is the colour that is just outside our vision at the red end of this scale. Infrared radiations can be used to detect sources of heat, and can also be used to take photographs of objects in the dark, provided that the objects are emitting some form of heat energy. (See also Ultraviolet.)

Light-year: A measure of distances in deep space. (See AU.) Light moves at a speed of 299,792 kilometres a second, and a light year is the distance that a beam of light would travel in a year.

Meteor: A 'meteoroid' that penetrates the Earth's

atmosphere, but does not reach the surface. Usually meteors are very small, and only become visible when they plunge into the Earth's atmosphere, and burn up in the intense heat that is generated by the friction between themselves and the air that they are travelling through.

Meteorite: A meteoroid that actually manages to penetrate the atmosphere and fall to the surface of the Earth. These are very rare, but of considerable interest to scientists because they give us clues as to how our solar system was formed.

Meteoroid: A piece of dust or rock floating around in space. Sometimes these are the remains of comets that have disintegrated; sometimes they are pieces from asteroids. Often it is impossible to tell where they have come from.

Nebula: A cloud of gas and dust in space caused by the past explosion of a star. These are outside the solar system, and cover huge areas of space.

Nova: A star, usually very faint, that suddenly flares up, and becomes thousands of times brighter. It stays bright for a time, and then gradually fades away until it is the same as it was when it started. Some novae will do this on a number of occasions, and are called recurrent novae. The cause is a great upheaval in the material of which the star is made. Important novae include Nova Persei (1901), Nova Aquilae (1918), Nova Herculis (1934), Nova Delphini (1967) and Nova Cygni (1975). It is not possible to predict when one is about to happen.

(See also Supernova.)

Nucleus: The solid head of a comet, reckoned to consist of a mixture of dust and frozen gases, that travels on an elliptical path through space. It is only when the nucleus gets comparatively close to the Sun that it forms the coma, which makes up the head of the comet, and the tail, which completes the picture of a comet as we usually imagine it.

Occultation: Something that happens when an apparently large body in space, for example the Moon, moves in front of an apparently much smaller body, for example one of the planets.

Orbit: The path through space that is taken by a body under the influence of the gravity of another body. The Earth orbits the Sun, and the Moon orbits the Earth.

Perihelion: The point in the orbit of a comet when it is nearest to the Sun, and just about to start its journey out into space again. It is the opposite end to the aphelion.

Period: The amount of time between the recurrences of comets and other astronomical phenomena.

Planet: A mass of material that is in orbit around a star, which is not usually a source of radiant energy in its own right. Planets may reflect the light from a star, but usually they are very difficult to detect. Nobody really knows how many planets there are outside our own solar system, nor what the chances are of finding life on any of them. There are a number of theories about the chances of finding life on other planets, but there is not yet any proof.

Plasma: Electrically-charged particles of gas that glow. They are formed by the intense radiation of the Sun acting on bits of the comet that are blown off as it sublimes, and these particles form the outside part of a comet's tail, together with all the dust particles which form the inner or 'dust tail'. The plasma tail is straight. The dust tail can form a curve. If this happens it is possible to see the difference between the two tails.

Pulsar: A 'dark' star that is usually only detected because it gives off radio waves as it spins around. These can be picked up by radio telescopes.

Quasi-Stellar radio sources (Quasars): Stars, originally located by radio astronomers, which give out an enormous amount of energy for their size.

Radio telescope: A telescope that does not use light to pick up distant objects, but uses radio waves instead. It does not give a 'picture' in the normal sense of the word, but scientists are able to learn a great deal from the radio waves that its large aerials pick up.

Reflector: A term used to describe a type of telescope that uses curved mirrors to focus the object at which it is pointed. This is the best kind of astronomical telescope. It has the ability to magnify an object a great number of times without the image becoming coloured, which is the fault of refracting telescopes.

Refractor: A name given to a type of telescope that works on the principle that light waves are bent as they pass through transparent objects. You can see this for yourself if you put a straight stick into a glass of water; from some angles it will appear to have bent. A refracting telescope uses lenses – pieces of transparent glass with curved faces that bend the light and focus an image. Unfortunately, different wavelengths (colours) of light bend by different amounts, which on a cheap telescope means that the object at which you are looking will be surrounded by a fringe of different colours. Even on an expensive telescope it is not possible to get rid of this chromatic aberration completely, and the greater the magnification of the telescope the worse it will appear.

Satellite: A body that is on an orbital path around a planet. There are two types of satellite: natural ones, like our Moon and the moons of other planets, and artificial ones, which are manufactured on Earth and launched into an orbit by a rocket. Artificial satellites are used for all sorts of purposes, like predicting the weather, sending television programmes from one country to another, and even helping one country to spy on another. There are probably more than 2,000 artificial satellites orbiting the Earth at present.

Solar: Means 'related to the Sun'. The solar system

is the group of planets and their satellites that orbit around the sun.

Solar wind: Streams of electrically charged particles that are emitted by the Sun.

Sublime: To change straight from a solid to a gas without becoming a liquid in between. Some materials possess this property; e.g. the nucleus of a comet sublimes, and the gases produced turn into the plasma tail of the comet.

Sunspot: A dark patch on the surface of the Sun, caused by an enormous 'storm' in the material of the Sun's surface. Sunspots move slowly across the face of the Sun, and can cause considerable disturbance on Earth, disrupting radio and television broadcasts. Their appearance is spasmodic, but their number reaches its maximum about once every eleven years.

Supernova: Similar in many respects to a nova, but it can increase in brightness by many million times. It often marks the end of a star, and the beginning of a nebula.

Ultraviolet: The other, invisible, end of the light range that we cannot detect, the opposite of infrared. The Sun gives off a great deal of ultraviolet radiation, which could be very harmful to us. Fortunately, most of it is filtered out by the ozone layer of the Earth's atmosphere. Although ultraviolet light is invisible to man, it can be seen by many insects.

Universe: Literally, everything in space. All the stars, planets, galaxies and constellations, and anything that can be found anywhere.

Zenith: The point in the heavens directly above the head of an observer. A useful point to remember, because it is often used in indicating whereabouts to look for an object in space. Not quite so useful is the nadir, which is the point of the heavens directly below the feet of an observer – in other words on the other side of the Earth!

Further Reading

There have been a great number of books written on astronomy, from very simple ones for very young children to extremely complicated ones dealing with a single subject in great depth. The ones that I have suggested are of general interest.

The Yearbook of Astronomy, published by Sidgwick and Jackson Ltd.

The Guinness Book of Astronomy Facts and Figures, published by Guinness Superlatives.

A Dictionary of Astronomy by Dr Robert Maddison, published by Hamlyn.

Your Book of Astronomy by Patrick Moore, published by Faber.

The Young Astronomer by Sheila Snowden, published by Usborne.

The Young Astronomer's Handbook by James Muirden, published by Pan.

Useful Addresses and Places to Visit

Listed below are a number of addresses that you will find useful if you are interested in furthering your studies of astronomy. However, the list is by no means comprehensive and, for reasons of space, only a few astronomical societies outside those of Great Britain are given a mention. As suggested earlier, if you would like to know more about astronomical organisations within your country, then contact your national astronomical society (if you have one) to see if they can help you or check for addresses in your telephone directory or at your local library.

Great Britain

With most of the addresses given below, it is as well to telephone before going to visit them, as they are not all open all the time.

The British Astronomical Association
Burlington House,
Piccadilly,
London. W1
(Telephone: [01] 734 4145)

The Federation of Astronomical Societies,
19 Warren Road,
Kirkby in Ashfield,
Nottingham.

(This Federation does not publish a telephone number so you should write to them with your enquiry. They will be able to tell you whether there is an astronomical society in your area.)

The Junior Astronomical Society,
22 Queensthorpe Road,
London. SE26 4PH

Open to interested beginners of any age. Meets four times a year at Holborn Library, London WC1. A quarterly magazine and a bi-monthly newsletter are sent to members.

The Royal Greenwich Observatory,
Herstmonceux Castle,
Sussex.
(Telephone: [0323] 833171)

The Old Royal Observatory,
Greenwich Park,
London. SE10
(Telephone: [01] 858 1167)

Open winter 9.00 a.m. to 5.00 p.m. Tuesday to
Saturday; 2.00 p.m. to 5.00 p.m. Sunday
Open summer 10.00 a.m. to 6.00 p.m. Tuesday to
Saturday; 2.00 p.m. to 5.30 p.m. Sunday

The Planetarium,
Marylebone Road,
London. W1
(Telephone: [01] 486 1121)

Open Monday to Sunday 11.00 a.m. to 4.30 p.m.
Presentations every hour. Telephone for details of
the programme.

The Science Museum,
Exhibition Road,
South Kensington,
London. SW7
(Telephone: [01] 589 3456)

Open 10.00 a.m. to 6.00 p.m. Monday to Saturday;
2.30 p.m. to 6.00 p.m. Sunday. Closed Bank Holidays.

The Geological Museum,
Exhibition Road,
South Kensington,
London. SW7
(Telephone: [01] 589 3444)

Open 10.00 a.m. to 6.00 p.m. Monday to Saturday;

2.30 p.m. to 6.00 p.m. Sunday. Exhibitions on the Story of the Earth and the Origins of the Universe.

Australia
The Astronomical Society of Australia,
c/o The Astronomy Department,
University of Sydney,
Sydney,
New South Wales,
Australia 2006.

Canada
The Canadian Astronomical Society,
(President: Dr John Mcleod)
5071 West Saanich Road,
R.R.5,
Victoria,
British Columbia,
Canada.
V8X 4M6

New Zealand
The Royal Astronomical Society of New Zealand,
Executive Secretary,
P.O. Box 3181,
Wellington,
New Zealand.

South Africa
The Astronomical Society of South Africa,
P.O. Box 9,
Observatory,
7935 Cape,
South Africa.

United States of America
The American Astronomical Society,
c/o Dr Peter B Boyce,
1816 Jefferson Place NW,
Washington DC 20036,
U.S.A.